PIANO • VOCAL • GUITAR

RADIOHEAD
THE KING OF LIMBS

Alfred

Produced by
Alfred Music Publishing Co., Inc.
P.O. Box 10003
Van Nuys, CA 91410-0003
alfred.com

Printed in USA.

ISBN-10: 0-7390-8140-3
ISBN-13: 978-0-7390-8140-2

Arranged by Olly Weeks; Edited by Lucy Holliday
Designed by Stanley Donwood; Faber Music Artwork by The Ghost

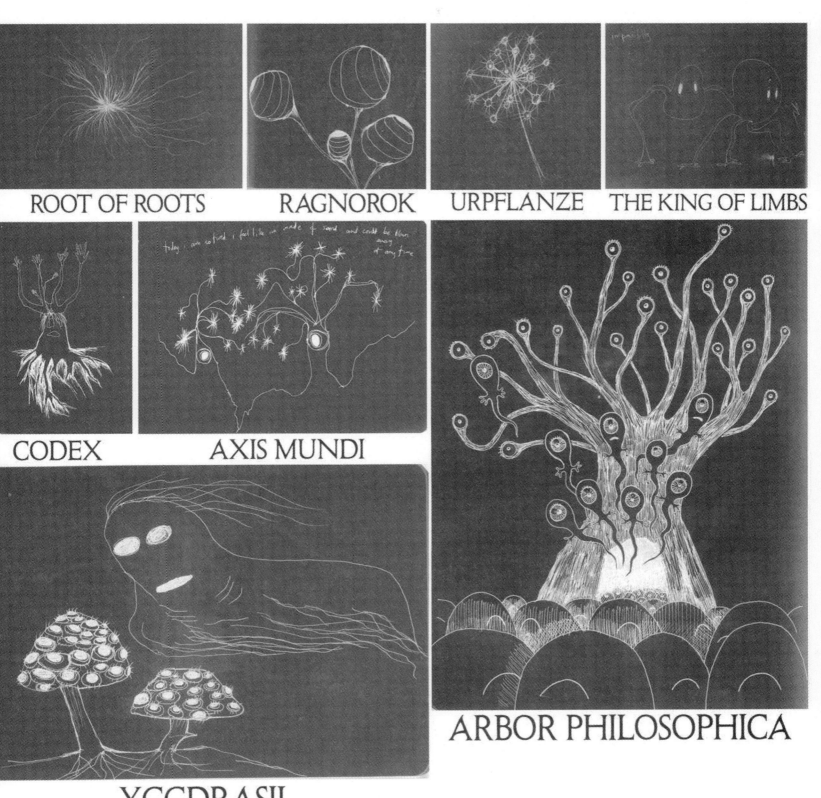

ROOT OF ROOTS RAGNOROK URPFLANZE THE KING OF LIMBS

CODEX AXIS MUNDI

ARBOR PHILOSOPHICA

YGGDRASIL

BLOOM

Words and Music by Thom Yorke, Jonathan Greenwood, Colin Greenwood, Edward O'Brien and Philip Selway

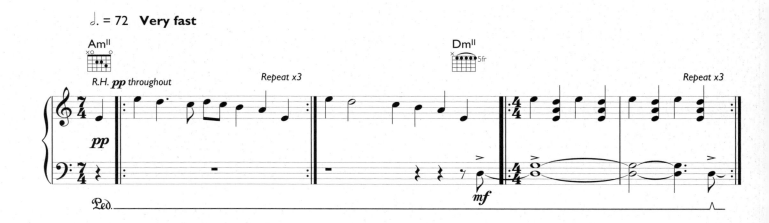

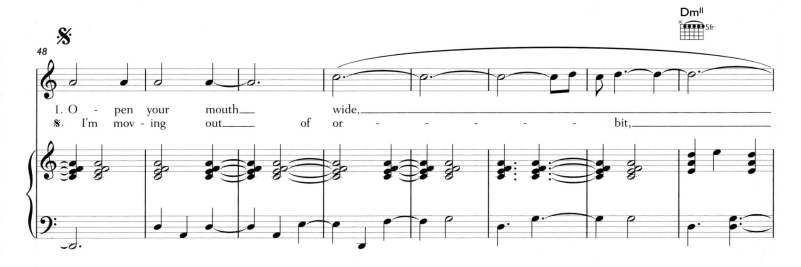

1. O - pen your mouth___ wide,_____

%. I'm mov - ing out___ of or - - - - - bit,_____

a u - ni - ver - sal sigh,_____

turn - ing in som - er - saults,_____

and while___ the o - cean blooms,_____
a gi - ant tur - tles___ eyes,_____

it's what keeps me___ a - live._____
a jel - ly - fish___ float by._____

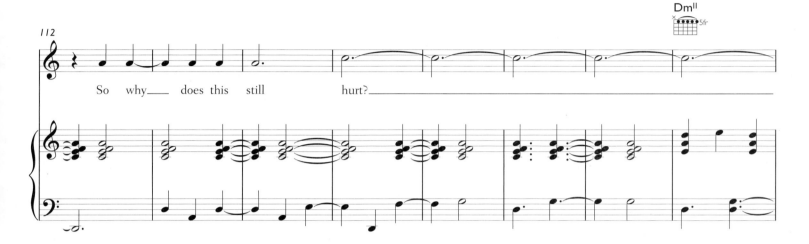

So why__ does this still hurt?_____

(Small notes 2° only)

(It's what keeps me_____ a - live.)_____

(Sing 1° only)

Don't blow__ your mind__ with why._____

To Coda ⊕

Ooh,_____

— ooh._____

Ped. (Keep pedal depressed until bar 221)

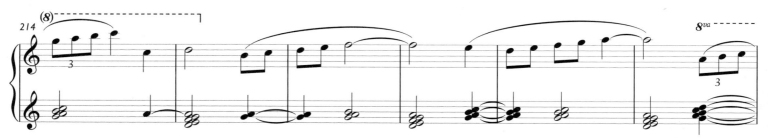

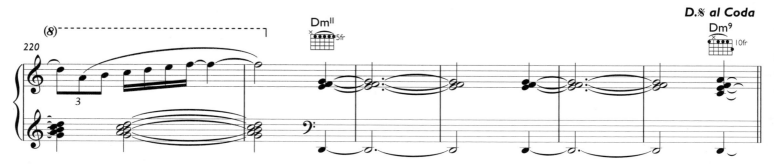

MORNING MR MAGPIE

Words and Music by Thom Yorke, Jonathan Greenwood, Colin Greenwood, Edward O'Brien and Philip Selway

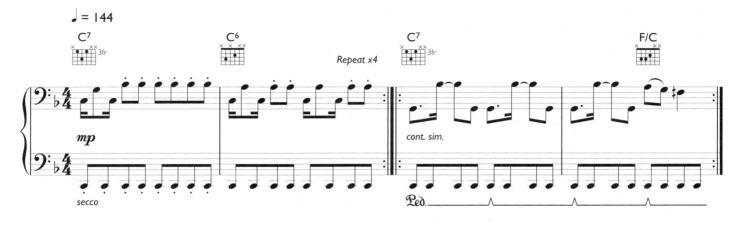

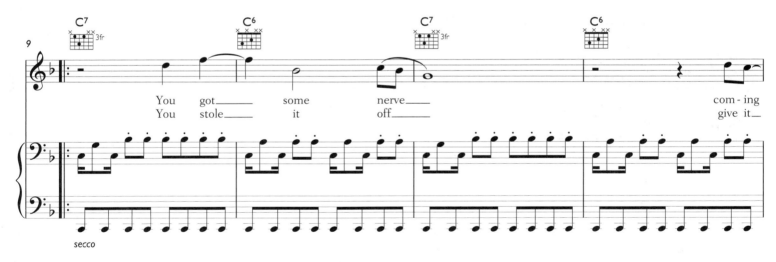

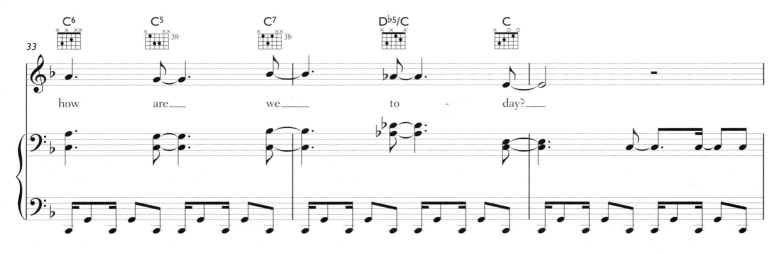

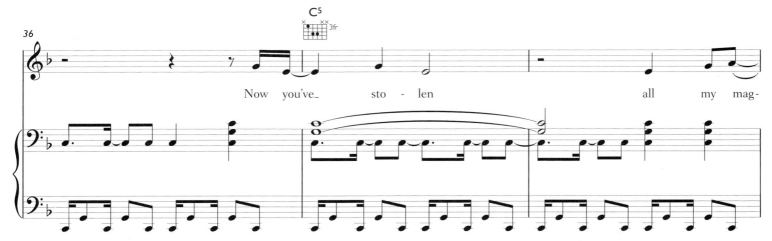

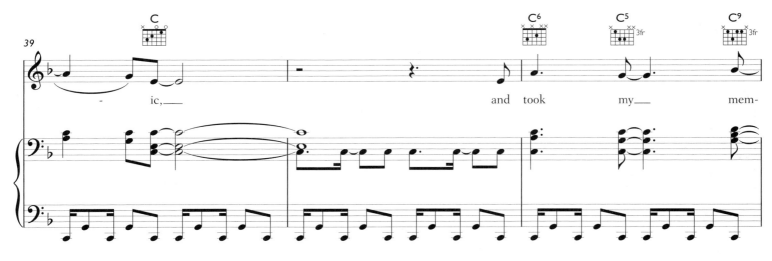

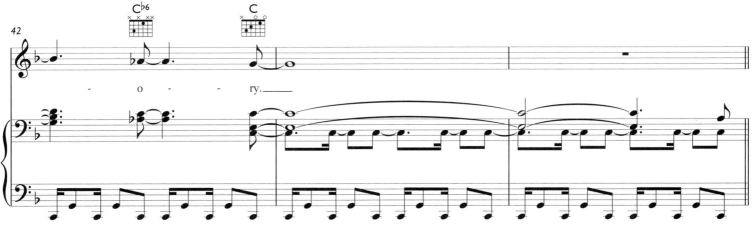

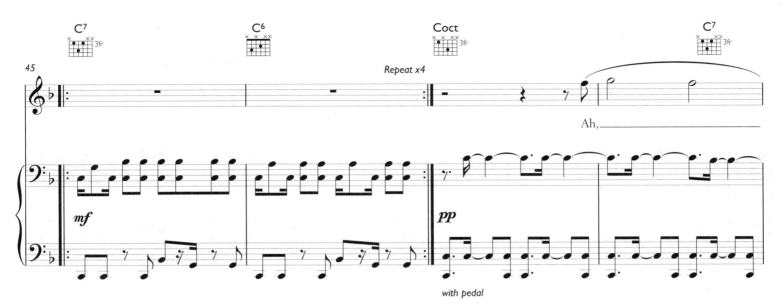

you know____ you should,____

but you____ don't.____

(Sing 1° only)

_mf_

Repeat ad lib. x3

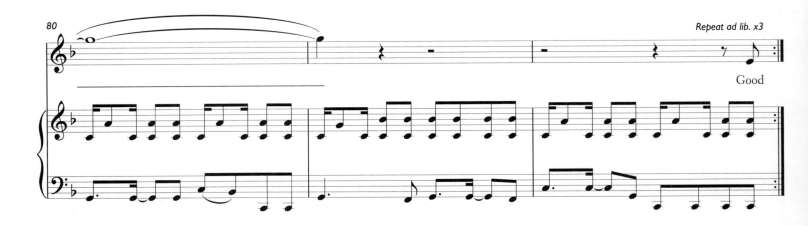

Good

morn - ing,___ Mis - ter Mag - pie,___

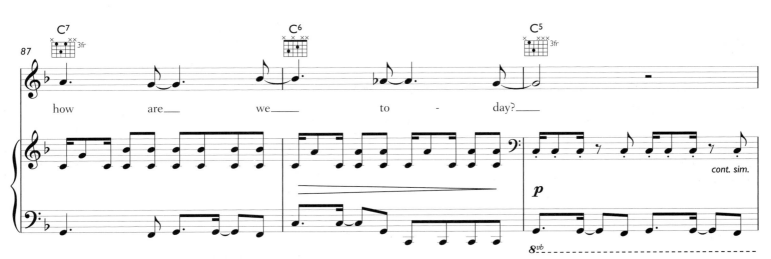

how are___ we___ to - day?___

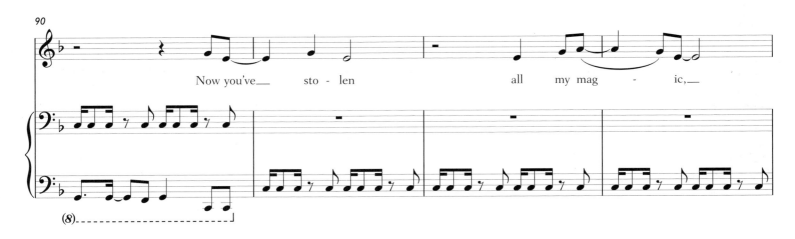

Now you've___ sto - len all my mag - ic,___

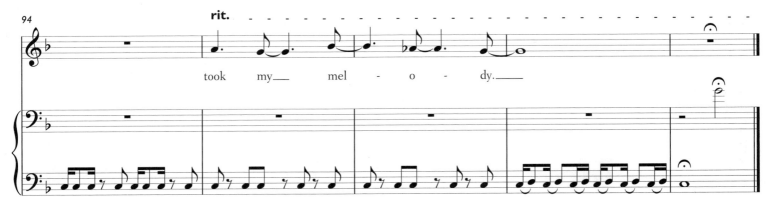

took my___ mel - o - dy.___

LITTLE BY LITTLE

Words and Music by Thom Yorke, Jonathan Greenwood, Colin Greenwood, Edward O'Brien and Philip Selway

♩ = 116

Tune guitar:
6 = D (lowest string)

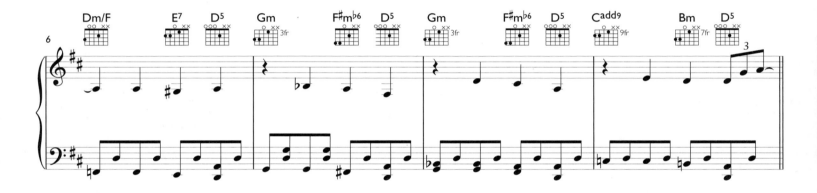

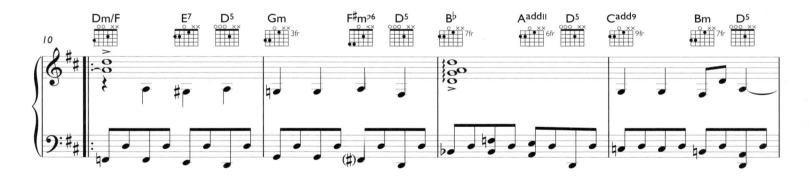

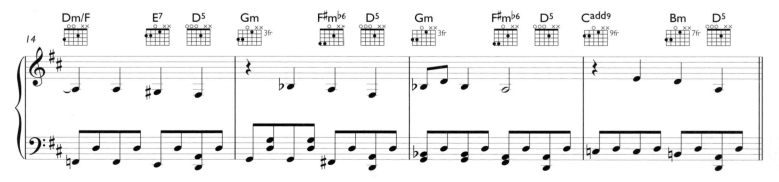

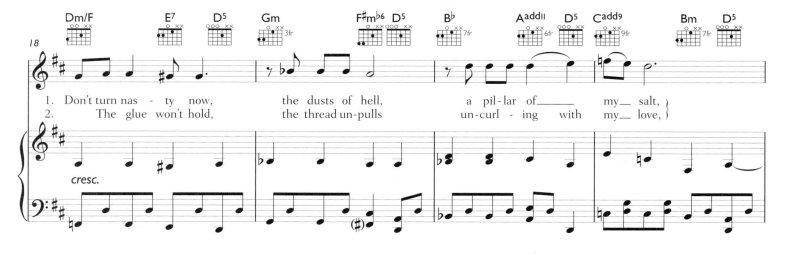

1. Don't turn nas - ty now, the dusts of hell, a pil-lar of_____ my__ salt,
2. The glue won't hold, the thread un-pulls un-curl - ing with my__ love,

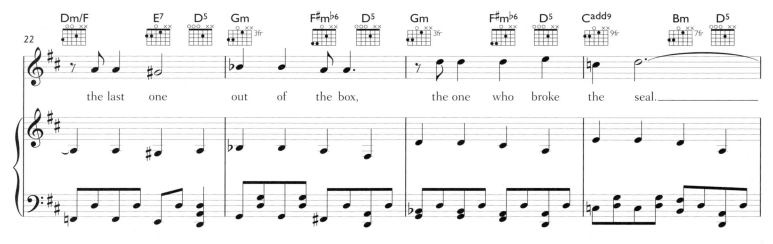

the last one out of the box, the one who broke the seal._____

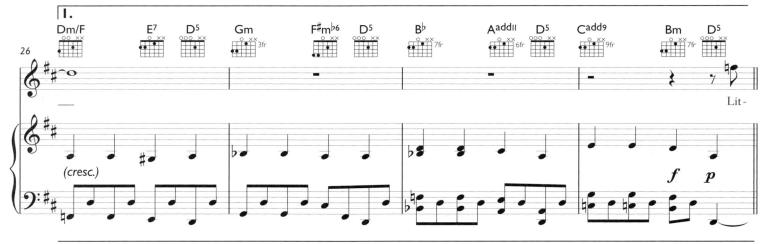

— Lit-

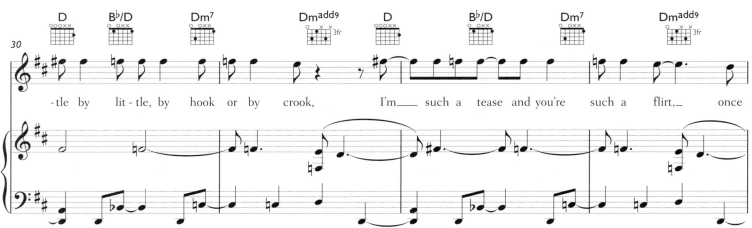

-tle by lit-tle, by hook or by crook, I'm__ such a tease and you're such a flirt,__ once

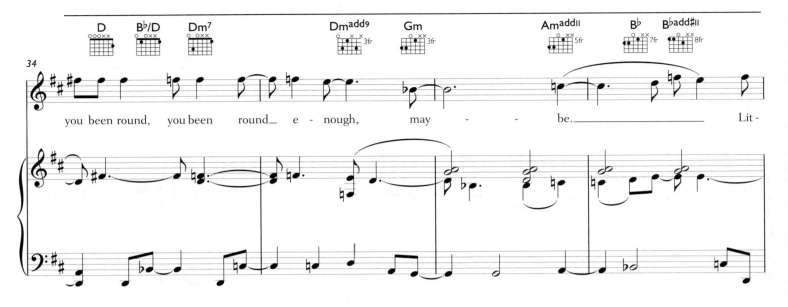

you been round, you been round_ e - nough, may - - be._____ Lit-

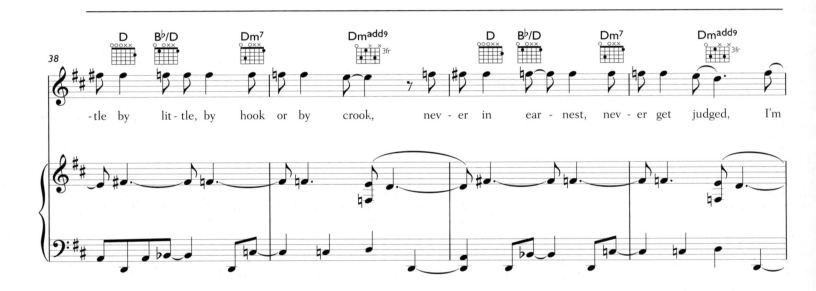

-tle by lit - tle, by hook or by crook, nev - er in ear - nest, nev - er get judged, I'm

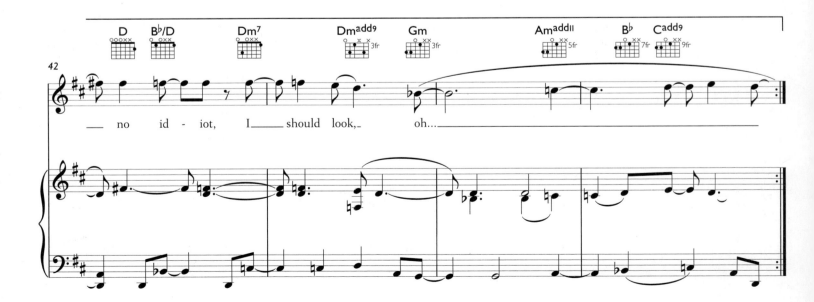

___ no id - iot, I ___ should look,_ oh._____

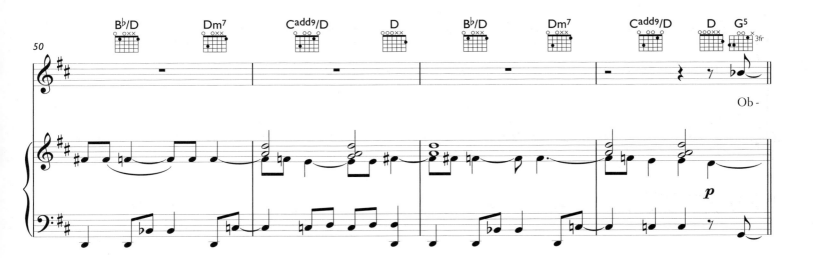

Ob -

-li - ga - tions,_____ com -
rou - tines_____ and sche - dules,_____ the drug_

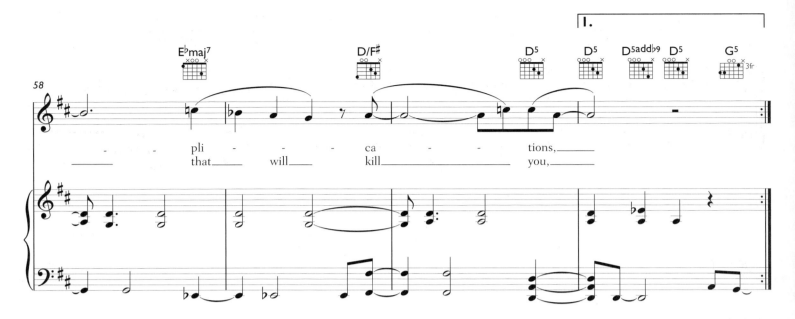

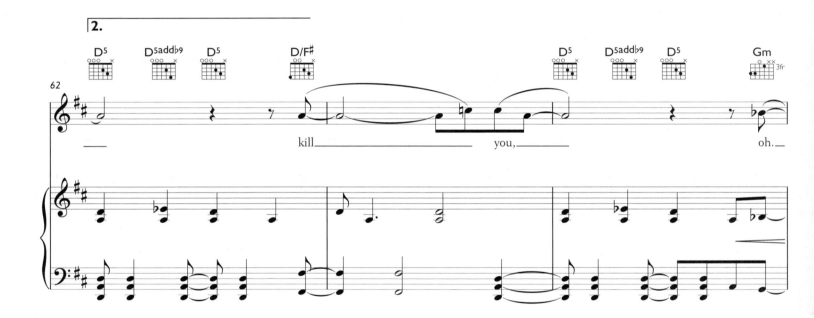

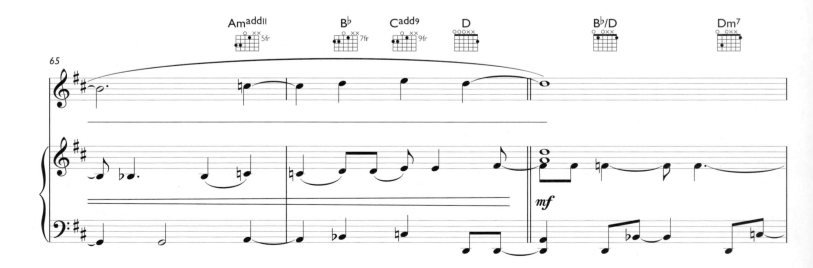

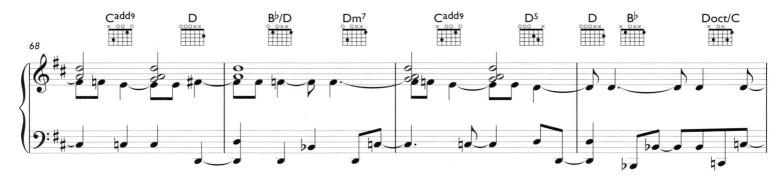

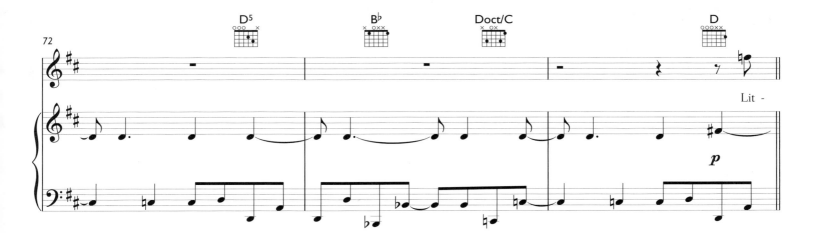

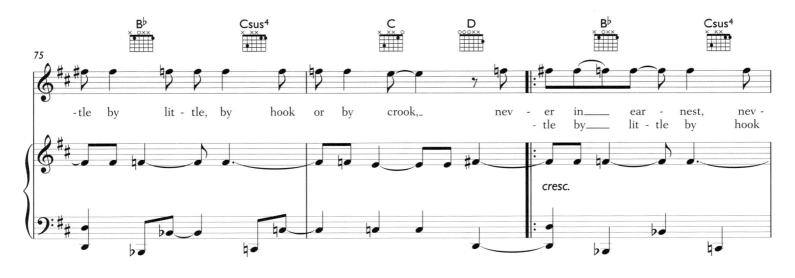

-tle by lit - tle, by hook or by crook,_ nev - er in___ ear - nest, nev-
-tle by___ lit - tle by hook

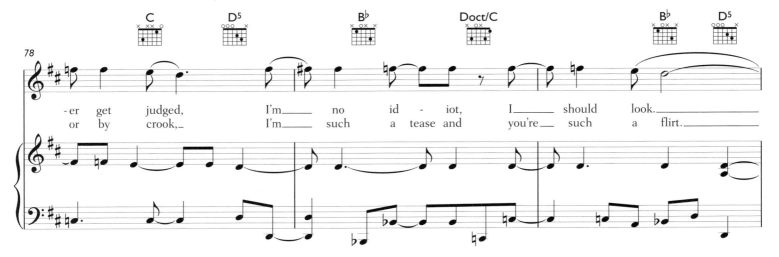

-er get judged, I'm___ no id - iot, I___ should look.___
or by crook,_ I'm___ such a tease and you're___ such a flirt.___

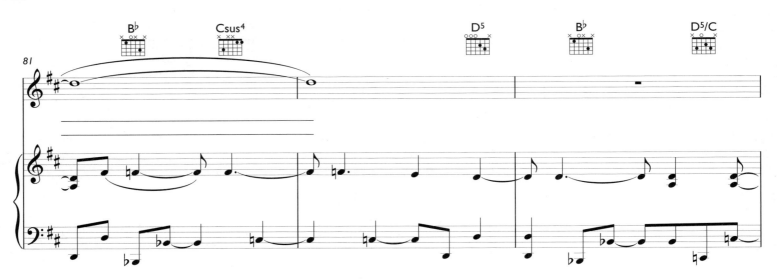

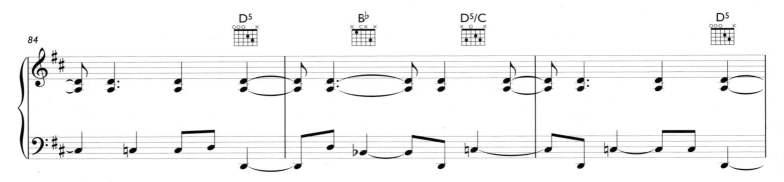

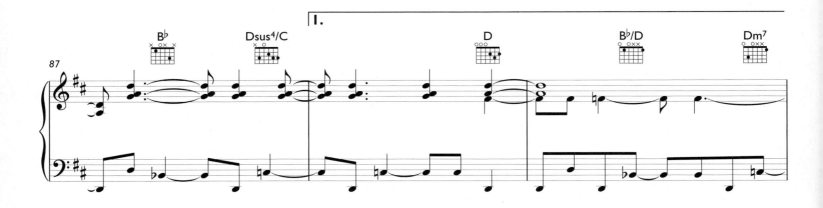

Lit -

FERAL

Words and Music by Thom Yorke, Jonathan Greenwood, Colin Greenwood, Edward O'Brien and Philip Selway

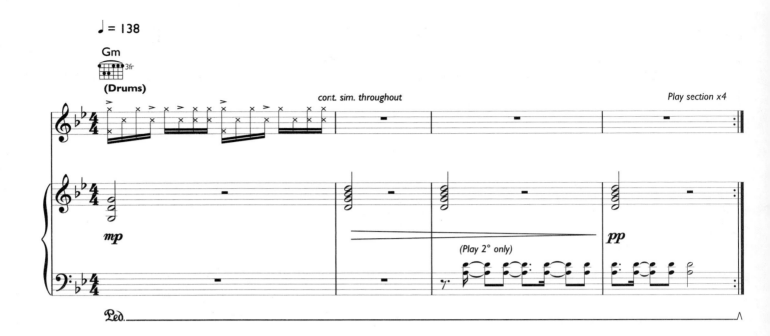

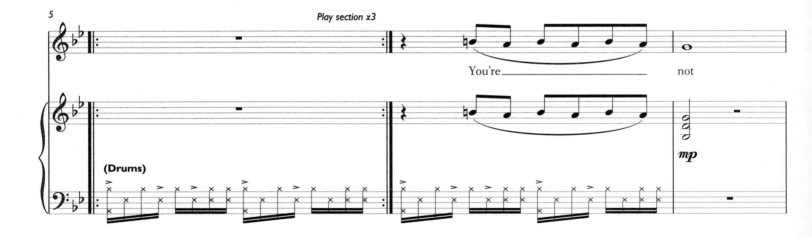

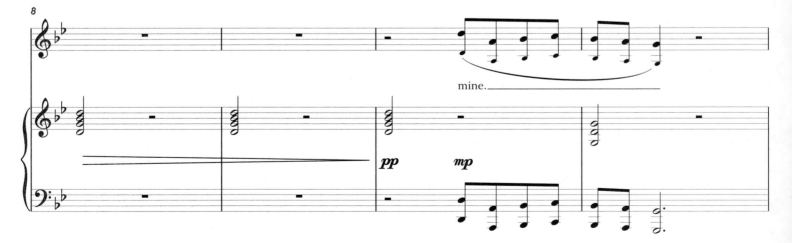

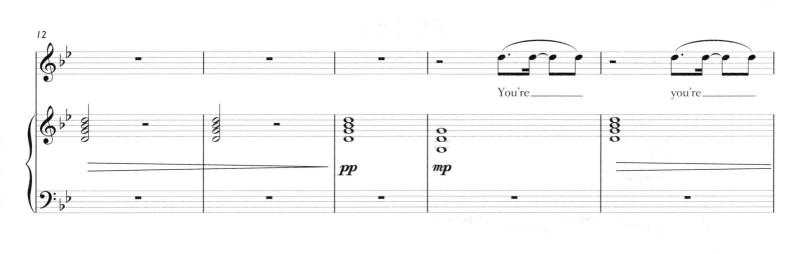

You're_____ you're_____

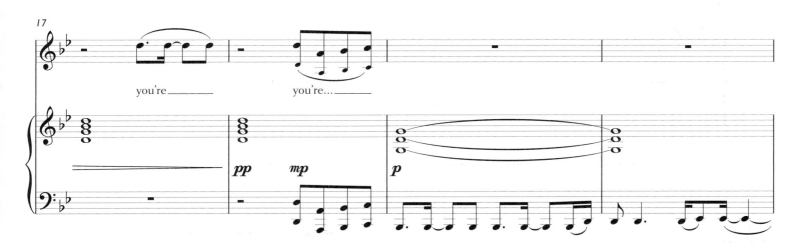

you're_____ you're..._____

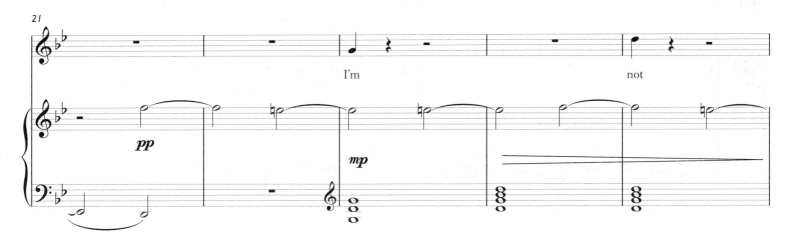

I'm not

yours.____ It's all____ fine, it's all____ fine, it's____

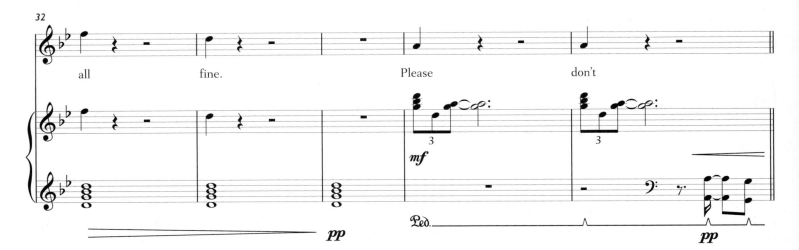

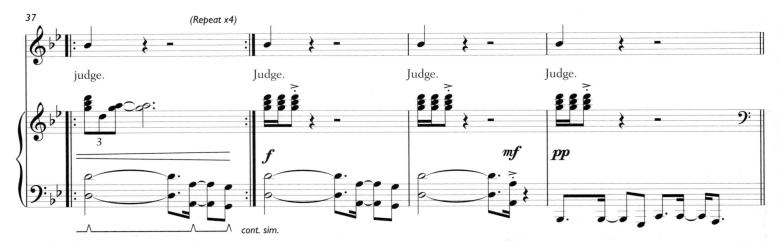

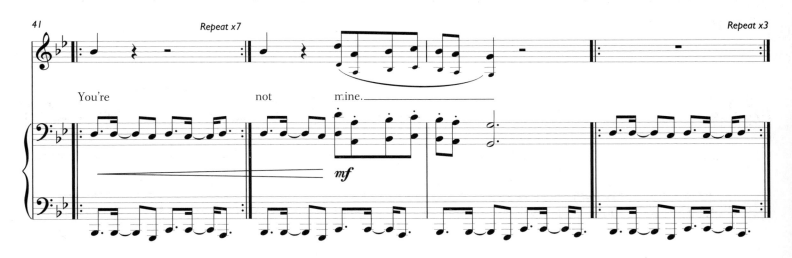

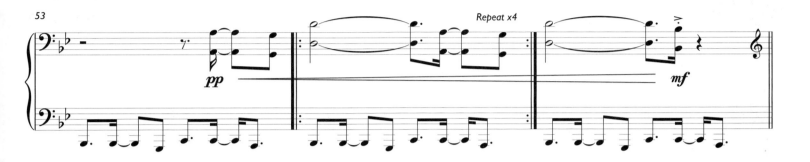

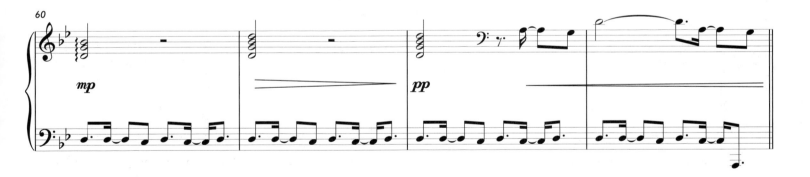

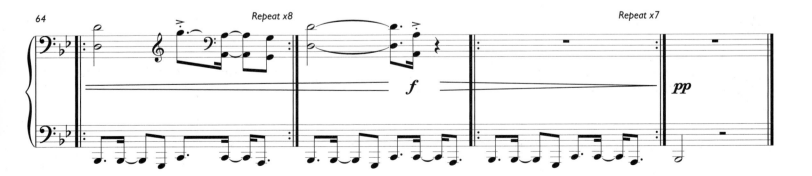

LOTUS FLOWER

Words and Music by Thom Yorke, Jonathan Greenwood, Colin Greenwood, Edward O'Brien and Philip Selway

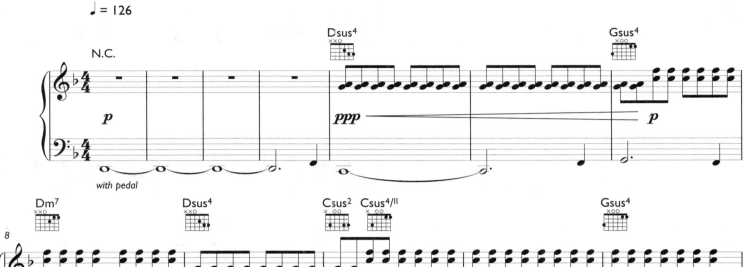

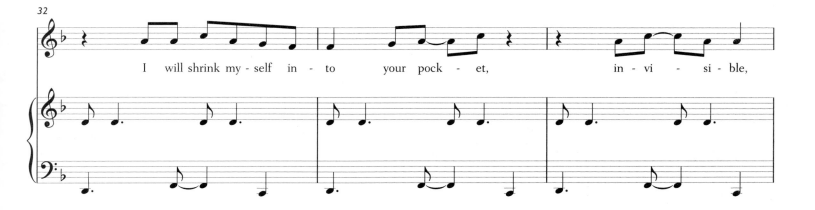

I will shrink my-self in - to your pock - et, in - vi - si - ble,

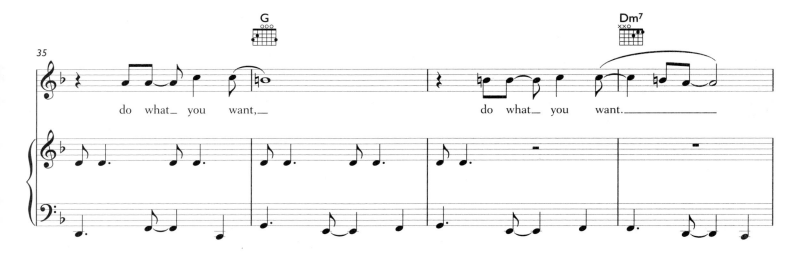

do what_ you want,_ do what_ you want._

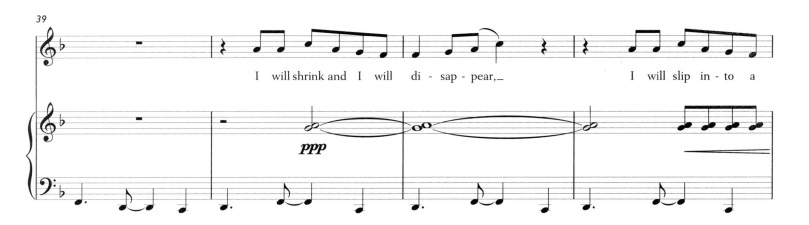

I will shrink and I will di - sap - pear,_ I will slip in - to a

groove and cut me off,_____ and cut__ me__ off._____

There's an

emp-ty space in-side my heart where the weeds take root so now I set you

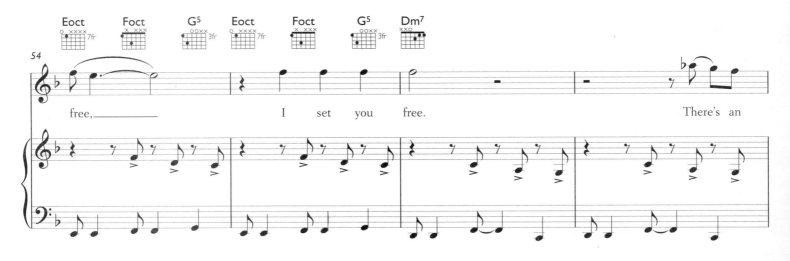

free,_____ I set you free. There's an

empty - ty space in - side my heart where the weeds take root, so now I set____ you

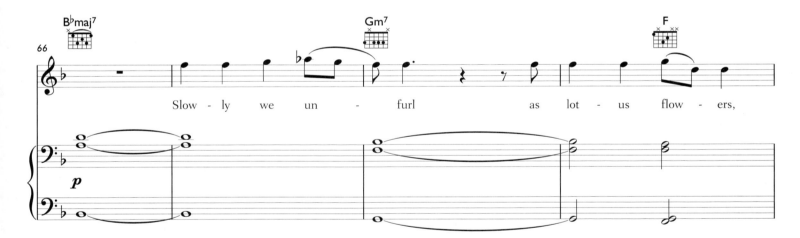

free,_____ I'll set you free.

Slow - ly we un - furl as lot - us flow - ers,

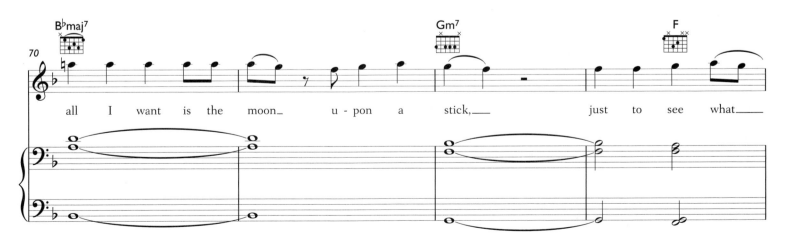

all I want is the moon__ u - pon a stick,____ just to see what____

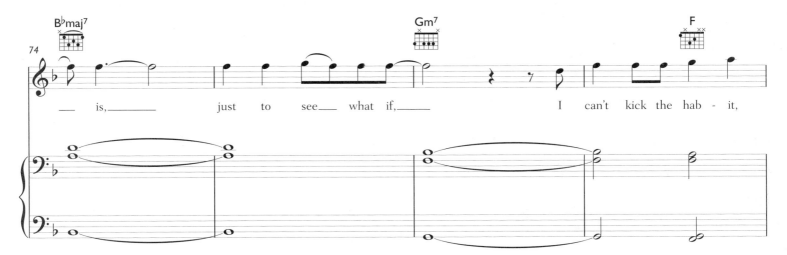

is,_____ just to see___ what if,_____ I can't kick the hab - it,

'just to feed your fast___ bal - loon - ing head.'___ 'Lis - ten to___ your heart.'

free,_____ I set you free.

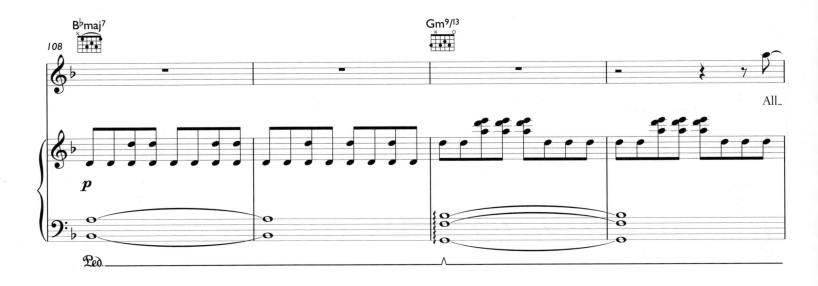

All_

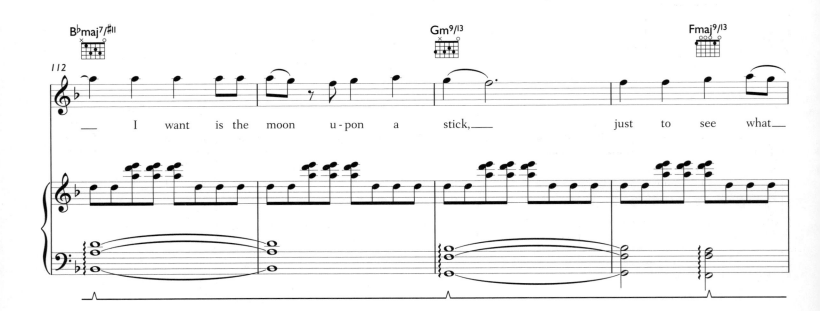

_ I want is the moon u-pon a stick,_____ just to see what_

pit, the dark - ness is___ be - neath,___ I can't kick your hab - it,

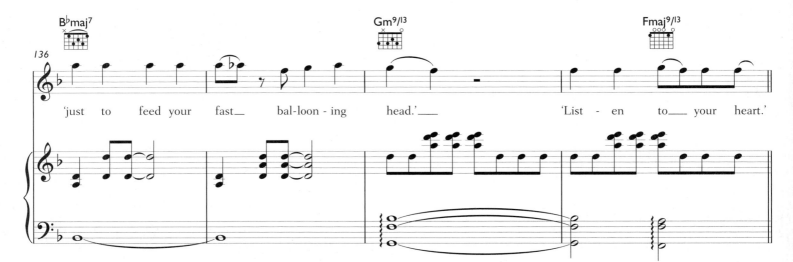

'just to feed your fast___ bal - loon - ing head.'___ 'List - en to___ your heart.'

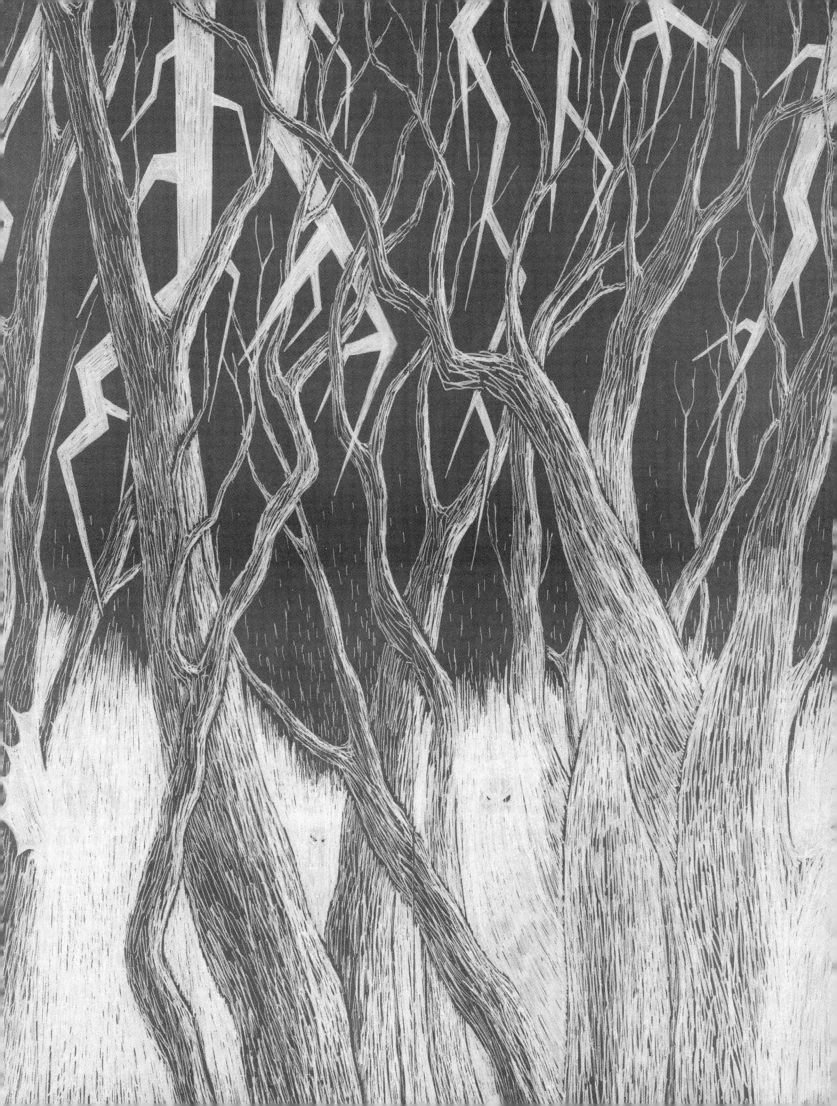

CODEX

Words and Music by Thom Yorke, Jonathan Greenwood, Colin Greenwood, Edward O'Brien and Philip Selway

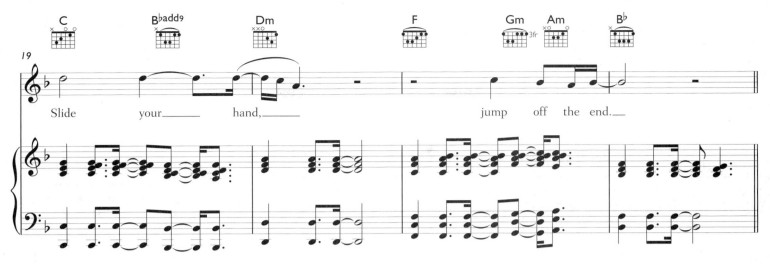

Slide your___ hand,___ jump off the end.___

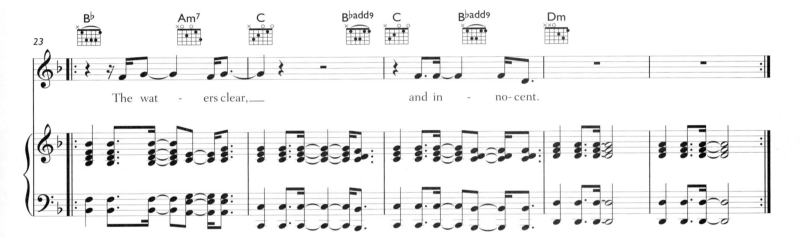

The wat - ers clear,___ and in - no-cent.

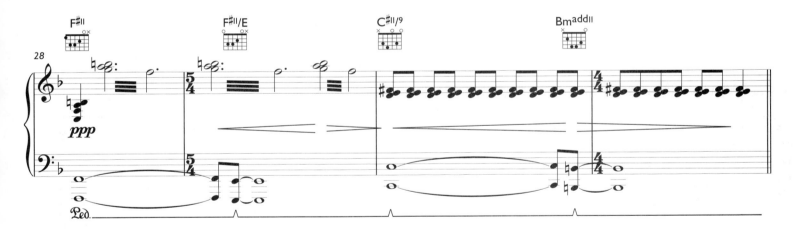

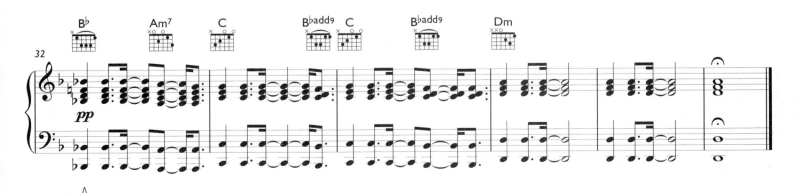

GIVE UP THE GHOST

Words and Music by Thom Yorke, Jonathan Greenwood, Colin Greenwood, Edward O'Brien and Philip Selway

in your arms,_____
into your arms,_____

in your arms._____
into your arms._____

Gath - er up_____ the pi -
Now I think_____ I've had____

-ti -_____ -ful_____
my_____ fill_____

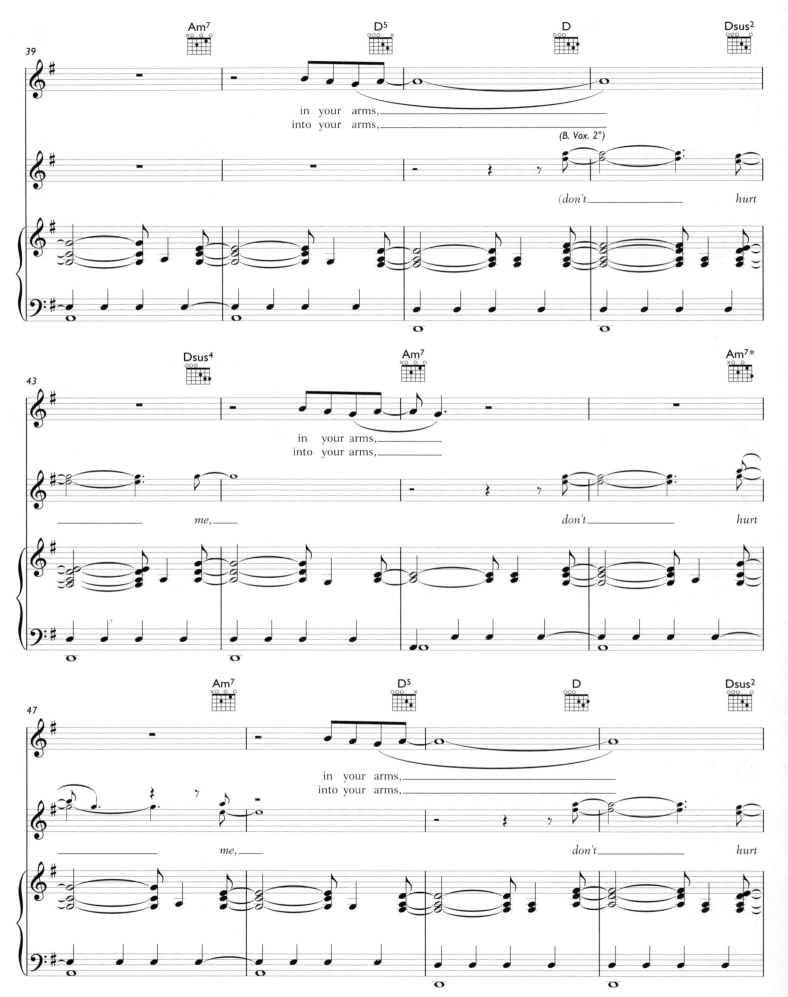

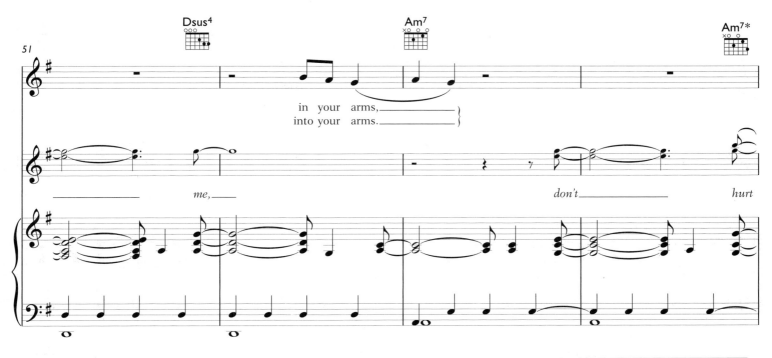

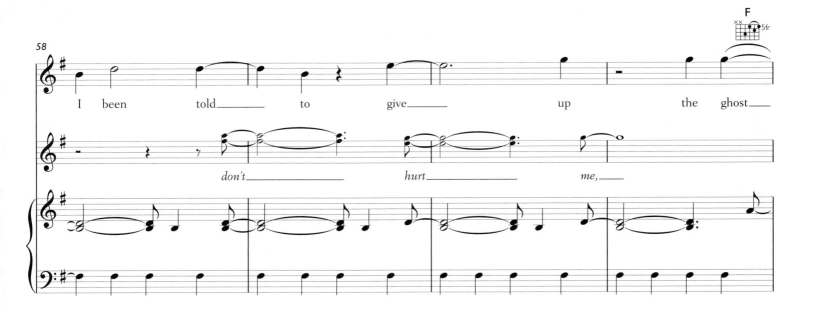

Repeat section x7 ad lib.

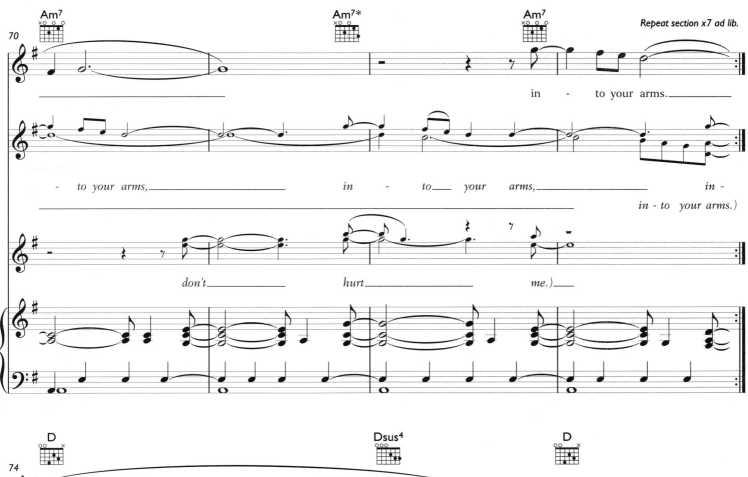

in - to your arms.

- to your arms, in - to your arms, in -
in - to your arms.)

don't hurt me.)

(fade to nothing)

(fade to nothing)

- to your arms, in - to your...)

SEPARATOR

Words and Music by Thom Yorke, Jonathan Greenwood, Colin Greenwood, Edward O'Brien and Philip Selway

It's like I've fall - en out of bed from a long and vi - vid dream,____ the sweet - est flo - wered fruits were hang - ing from the trees,____

fall-ing off a gi - ant bird that's been car-ry - ing me.___

It's like I've fall - en out of bed from a long and vi - vid dream.___ Just ex -

-act - ly___ as I___ re - mem - ber, ev - 'ry

word, ev - 'ry ges - ture, I've my

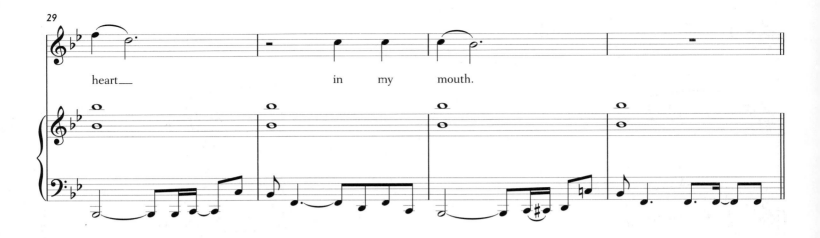

heart___ in my mouth.

Like I've fall - en out of bed from a long and vi - vid dream.___

Fin - al - ly I'm free of all the weight I've been car - ry - ing.___

(Oh,___

(Oh,___

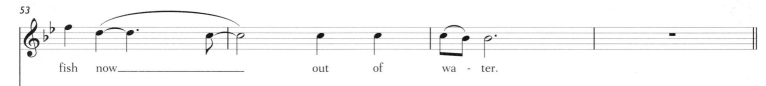

Fall-ing off a gi-ant bird that's been car-ry-ing me,_____

(Wake me up, wake me up,_____ up,_____ up,_____ up,_____
(Wake me_____ up...)

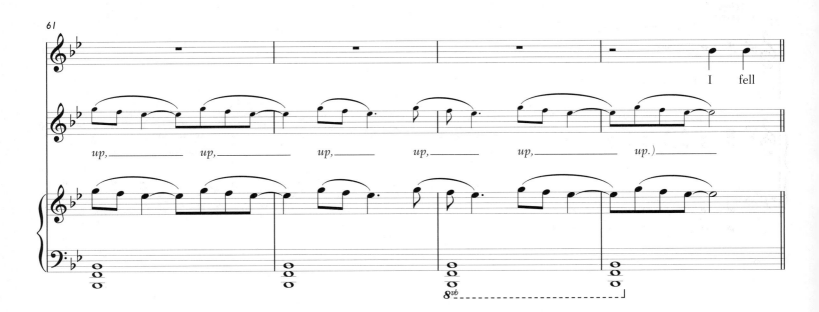

I fell

up,_____ up,_____ up,_____ up,_____ up,_____ up.)_____

o-pen, I fell un-der, at the

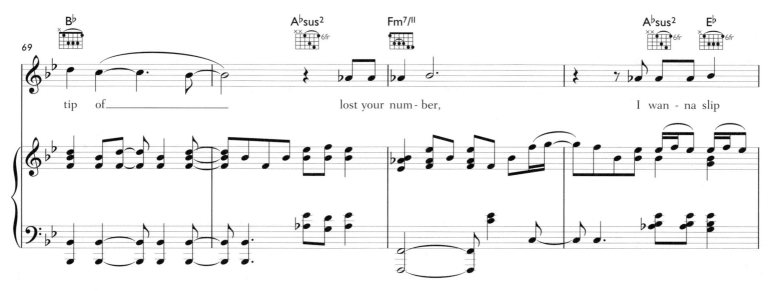

Wake me up, will you wake me up?

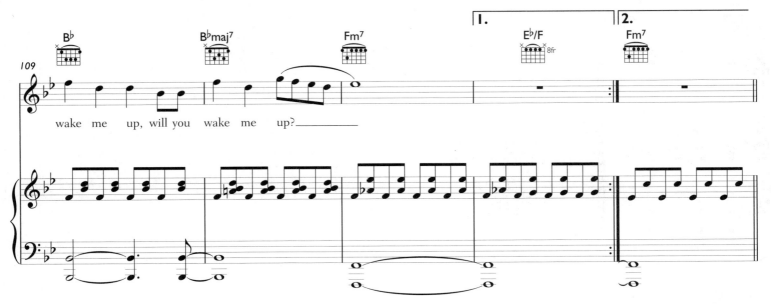

wake me up, will you wake me up?_____

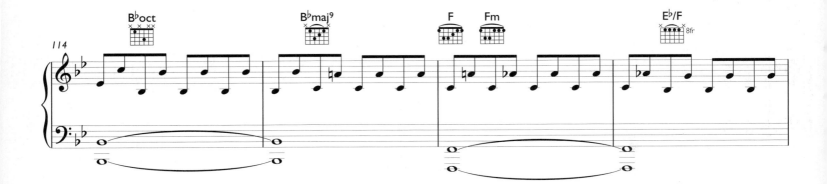

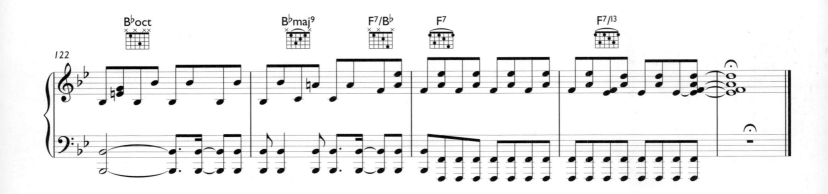